THE NAZARENES

By

Robert L. Gibson

authorHOUSE™

1663 LIBERTY DRIVE, SUITE 200
BLOOMINGTON, INDIANA 47403
(800) 839-8640
WWW.AUTHORHOUSE.COM

First published by AuthorHouse 02/28/05

ISBN: 1-4208-2687-5 (sc)

Printed in the United States of America
Bloomington, Indiana

This book is printed on acid-free paper.

ONE OF THE MOST IMPORTANT

MESSAGES I HAVE FOR YOU IS THAT

JESUS WAS A NAZARENE.

WHILE SOME PEOPLE KNOW THIS, IT IS

NOT WIDELY KNOWN. IT IS IMPORTANT

TO DISCUSS, BECAUSE IT CLARIFIES

MUCH IN THE NEW TESTAMENT. WHAT IS

A NAZARENE?

FIRST, RECALL THAT IT IS WRITTEN "HIS

PARENTS TOOK HIM TO NAZARETH,

BECAUSE IT WAS FORETOLD HE WOULD

BE A NAZARENE."

THIS DOESN'T MEAN A RESIDENT OF

NAZARETH, THE TOWN. IF IT DID, ALL

RESIDENTS OF THE TOWN WOULD BE

NAZARENES.

NO, IT DIDN'T MEAN THEY WERE

REGISTERING HIM AT NAZARETH FOR

THE STATE ORDERED CENSUS, OR HEAD

COUNT, FOR TAX PURPOSES.

A NAZARENE IS ONE SET APART,
ASKED TO TAKE AN OATH TO GOD. THE
NAZARENE SWEARS TO NEVER CUT HIS
HAIR. TO NEVER TOUCH THE DEAD. TO
NEVER INBIBE THE FRUIT OF THE VINE.
AS LONG AS HE KEEPS HIS OATH, HE IS
GRANTED SPECIAL POWERS FROM GOD.

THE FIRST JEWISH KING WAS SAUL. HE
ADMIRED SAMSON, AND PASSED THAT
ADMIRATION ON TO HIS PROTÉGÉ,
DAVID. DAVID OFCOURSE FATHERED
SOLOMAN, THE BLACK KING.

SAMSON WAS THE NAZARENE WE
EASILY RECOGNIZE AS ONE. HE HAD
THE POWER TO DEFEAT NUMBERS
OF PHILLISTINES, REMARKABLE
FIGHTING POWER, AND STRENGTH. HIS
PHILLISTINE ENEMIES RECOGNIZED HIM
AS A WOMANIZER, AND SET HIM UP WITH
DELILAH TO FIND HIS WEAKNESS, SO
AS TO DEFEAT HIM. SHE WENT THRU
SEVERAL ATTEMPTS TO QUESTION
HIM, UNTIL SHE FINALLY LEARNED HIS
POWER RESTED IN HIS HAIR. WHILE
HE SLEPT, SHE CUT HIS HAIR AND HE

BECAME POWERLESS. ENABLING HIS
EASY CAPTURE BY THE PHILLISTINES.

WHAT ELSE DO WE KNOW ABOUT A
NAZARENE?

WELL, WE DO KNOW THAT HE TELLS
RIDDLES THAT NEED TO BE FIGURED
OUT. TALES THAT OFTEN TEACH A
LESSON, PARABLES. SAMSON LOVED
HAVING PEOPLE TRY TO FIGURE OUT HIS
RIDDLES, SEVERAL OF WHICH STUMPED
DELILAH, AT FIRST. BEFORE HIS DEATH,

SAMSON WAS MADE A JUDGE OF THE
JEWS.

READ JUDGES FOR MORE DETAILS
ABOUT SAMSON'S RIDDLES, FOR
EXAMPLE, THE RIDDLE OF THE LION
AND HONEY.

THE JUDGES OF THE JEWS WERE
KNOWN AS THE SANHEDRIN, A BODY
LIKE OUR SUPREME COURT. JESUS'S
FATHER WAS A MEMBER OF THAT BODY.
TO BE A MEMBER WAS LIKENED TO
BEING A CHURCH LEADER AS WE HAVE

TODAY OUR COUNCILS NUMBERED
WITH DEACONS AND STEWARDS OF THE
FAITH. A MEMBER HAD TO BE OF A HIGH
STATION.

IT WAS SAID OF JESUS THAT HE WOULD
RETURN TO BE JUDGE OF THE QUICK
AND THE DEAD. THE LAST POSITION A
NAZARENE ROSE TO WAS JUDGE.

LET'S TAKE A LOOK AT THE NAZARENE
OATH. FIRST HE CAN'T CUT HIS HAIR,
CANNOT SHAVE. SO FORGET ALL
IMAGES OF JESUS WITHOUT A BEARD,

WITH CLOSE HAIRCUTS WHETHER IN ITALIAN OR GREEK PAINTINGS. ALSO FORGET RED HAIRED IRISH LOOKING JESUS. HE WAS A SEMITE, NOT A CELT.

LOOK FURTHER AT THE IMAGE OF MOSES. HE HAD A PRINCELY HOLY HAIR FACTOR OF THE ANCIENTS, BRAIDED HAIR. YOU SEE IT ON IMAGES OF PHAROAHS, EGYPTIAN OFFICERS, AS MOSES WAS, ALSO ON THE RABBI, AND ON ORTHODOX JEWS. EVEN RASTAFARIANS SEE THEIR BRAIDS BEING OF "JA", OR HOLY TO THEM.

ACCEPT THAT JESUS NEVER CUT HIS

HAIR, BUT RATHER WORE BRAIDS.

THAT HE NEVER SHAVED, OTHERWISE

HE WOULD, LIKE SAMSON, LOSE HIS

POWER.

NEXT, REMEMBER HE CANNOT

TOUCH THE DEAD. WHEN HE WOKE

HIS COMATOSE UNCLE LAZARUS, HE

SHOUTED "COME FORTH LAZARUS"

NEVER APPROACHING THE SEPULCRE

OR TOUCHING HIM. FINALLY AND MOST

IMPORTANTLY, HE WAS NEVER TO DRINK WINE, OR ANY PRODUCT OF THE VINE.

MISUNDERSTOOD IS THE STORY OF THE WEDDING THAT HIS MOTHER HOSTED. SHE RAN OUT OF WINE FOR THE GUESTS AND ONLY HAD JUGS OF WATER LEFT. IT IS WRITTEN THAT SHE ASKED HIM TO TURN THE WATER INTO WINE FOR THE GUESTS. HE REPLIED "BUT YOU KNOW MOTHER, IT IS NOT MY TIME." HE COMPLIED, BUT HIS PROTEST WAS NOT ABOUT USING HIS POWERS AHEAD OF TIME. IT WAS NOT THAT HE

WAS UNDERAGE AND FORBIDDEN TO
DEAL WITH DRINKS. IT WAS THAT HE
WAS NEVER TO INBIBE WINE. AS LONG
AS HE WAS TO KEEP HIS POWER.

SECONDLY, MUCH ADO AND SEVERAL
MOVIES AND BOOKS HAVE THE IDOL OF
HIS WINE GLASS AS A TREASURE TO BE
SOUGHT BY KNIGHTS, BY TREASURE
HUNTERS, BY CHURCH OFFICERS. THE
SEARCH FOR THE GOLDEN CHALISE.
THE WINE GLASS OF JESUS. USED AT
THE LAST SUPPER. WE NOW KNOW BY
MY WORK, THAT THIS IS RIDICULOUS.

WHILE HE HAD THE DISCIPLES DRINK

HIS WINE FROM TWO SEPARATE CUPS,

THE FORRUNNER OF COMMUNION, HE

DID NOT DRINK FROM THEM HIMSELF.

AS A JEW, HE WOULD FROWN ON ITEMS

BEING WORSHIPPED. I REPEAT, HE DID

NOT DRINK WINE FROM THE ELUSIVE

ICONS. YES THERE WERE TWO CUPS,

EACH OFFERED TO TOAST DIFFERENT

THINGS.

WELL, DID HE EVER DRINK WINE OR

THE FRUIT OF THE VINE? YES HE DID.

ON THE CROSS, HE ASKED FOR WATER

TO QUENCH HIS THIRST, JUST BEFORE

HE SAID "ELI ELI, BARACHTHANI ".YOU

SEE THE SOLDIERS GAVE HIM GALL

TO DRINK. A VINEGAR DRINK. MADE

FROM THE VINE. IT INCREASES AND

EXASCERBATES THIRST. IT ALSO ENDED

HIS NAZARENE OATH.

NOT FINISHED WITH THIS. HE DID NOT

SAY MY FATHER, MY FATHER, WHY HAVE

YOU ABANDONED ME?

THE REAL TRANSLATION IS "MY POWER,

MY POWER! IT HAS LEFT ME!" THOUGH

EL IS THE NAME OF GOD, IT IS ONLY
ONE TRANSLATION OF ELI.

THE STAR OF BETHLEHEM

THIS IS ONE OF MY FAVORITES. ONE OF
MY ORIGINAL DISCOVERIES.

THE WISE MEN IN A SONG WE SING "WE
THREE KINGS OF ORIENT ARE" THERE
IS A CLUE. CHINESE SCHOLARS KNEW
ABOUT THE STAR BEFORE IT HAPPENED.
THEY WERE AWARE IT COMES EVERY SO
OFTEN.

WHILE MOST JEWS SOUGHT TO

DISTANCE THEMSELVES FROM STAR

STUDY AND SUNWORSHIPPERS, AS

IT WAS NOT ALLOWED BY THE TEN

COMMANDMENTS, OTHERS WATCHED

THE SKIES, SOUGHT MEANING IN THEM.

THEY LEARNED THAT THE BEST TIME

TO PLANT AND TO HARVEST COULD BE

READ IN THE STARS. THEY GAVE THEM

MUCH MORE MEANING, AS YOU WILL

READ. IT WAS PARTLY UNAVOIDABLE

AS IS THE CULTURAL BENT OF TALKING

OF THE HEART WHEN THE BRAIN

IS IN CHARGE OF EMOTIONS. IT IS

PARTLY VERY USEFULL TO THOSE WHO

ARE OPPRESSED AND MUST REMAIN

SECRETIVE.

IT WOULD HELP TO VISIT THE

PLANETARIUM TO SEE WHAT MAGIC CAN

BE IMBUED IN THE STARS, ESPECIALLY

WHEN MUSIC AND UNDERSTANDING CAN

BE ADDED.

ONE OF THE LIGHTS YOU MAY SEE

THERE WOULD BE SATURN. THE

PLANET WITH THE HALO. THE PLANET
REPRESENTING THE JEWS.

ANOTHER LIGHT YOU MAY SEE IS THE
GREAT BIG POWERFUL JUPITER. IT
REPRESENTS THE HORNED POWERS
BABYLON, ROME AND THOSE
WHO OPPRESSED THE JEWS. THE
CONSTELLATIONS OR DOTS IN THE SKY
WERE ASSIGNED NAMES OF PIESCES
FOR THE JEWS AND TAURUS (THE
BULL,WITH HORNS) FOR JUPITER. IT
WAS FORETOLD BY SOOTHESAYERS
THAT THE CONJUNCTION OF THESE

CONSELLATIONS IN THE SKY, WOULD
SIGNAL THE COMING OF A HERO TO THE
JEWS TO FIGHT AND CONFRONT THE
TAURUS PEOPLE, A MESSIAH. A PERSON
COMBINING KING AND HEAD RABBI.

RECALL THAT PAUL AND OTHER
DISCIPLES WOULD DRAW A FISH IN THE
SAND TO SIGNAL HE WAS A NAZARENE,
TO OTHERS, SECRETLY.

THE FISH SIGN YOU SEE ON THE BACK
OF CAR TRUNKS COMES FROM PISCES.
ON THE CONTRARY. THE SYMBOL

OF THE HORNS IS IN FRONT OF
BABYLONIAN PALACES, WORN BY THEIR
HOLY BULLS, ALSO WORN BY SATAN.

EVERY EIGHT HUNDRED YEARS OR SO,
THE PLANETS LINE UP WITH PISCES
CONFRONTING TAURUS. AT THAT TIME
THE SKIES ARE LIT UP FOR OVER A
MONTH AT NIGHT. THE CHINESE (MEN
OF THE ORIENT) KNEW THIS FOR AGES.
FORGIVE ME IF THE RECURRANCE
CENTURIES IS NOT 800.PERHAPS
IT REPLACED MY MEMORY OF THE
RECUURANCE YEARS BECAUSE JESUS

NUMBER IS 800 (OR 888). RECALL THAT THE ENEMY HAS A NUMBER OF 666. AOUND THE TIME OF 600 ISRAEL SUFFERED ONE OF IT'S WORST DESTRUCTIONS BY THE ENEMY, THE ROMANS.

BUT I DIGRESS, THE CONJUNCTION OF THE THREE BODIES IN THE SKY : SATURN, JUPITER AND THE NORTH STAR, WERE WHAT THE STAR OF BETHLEHEM WAS. VERY BRIGHT IN THE NIGHT SKY. LASTING LONG ENOUGH TO ENABLE NIGHT TRAVEL.

NUMBERS ARE FASCINATING POINTS OF
THE BIBLE. YOU NEED NOT STUDY THE
CABALLA TO SEE SOME SIGNIFICANCE,
ONLY STUDY AND COMPARE. THE
WORLD WAS MADE IN SEVEN DAYS.
JESUS'S NUMBER IS 8. WHEN HE
RETURNS, IT WILL BE A DIFFERENT
WORLD.

MIRIAM

WHEN HEROD WAS APPOINTED KING
OF JUDAH, ISRAEL AND SOME OF THE

ENVIRONS, BY CAESAR OF ROME, HE

ENDEAVORED TO SEAL AND ESTABLISH

HIS SEAT WITH THE INHABITANTS.

HE DID SO BY MARRYING INTO THE

FAMILY OF ONE OF THE MOST BLUE

BLOOD AROUND, THE FAMILY OF THE

HASMONEANS, HE BUILT THE JEWS A

TEMPLE.

THE BRIDE HE CHOSE WAS THE

BEAUTIFUL MIRIAM, DAUGHTER OF AN

HASMONEAN. THE HASMONEANS HAD

RULED FOR DECADES PRIOR.

TEARS OF JOY MUST HAVE WELLED IN
JEWISH EYES TO HEAR THIS. THE LINE
WOULD AGAIN BE HASMONEAN. SHE
WAS A DESCENDANT OF THE FAMILY
OF JUDAS MACCABEUS, THE HERO OF
HONOUR WHO INSPIRED THE RELIGIOUS
HOLIDAY NEAR OUR CHRISTMAS
TIME. ONE OF THE BIGGEST JEWISH
HEROES NOT SPOKEN OF IN OUR BIBLE.
TWO CHAPTERS OF HIS NAME ARE
ELIMINATED FROM OUR BIBLE. A PRIEST,
HE AND HIS BROTHERS WERE ONE
OF THE FEW GROUPS OF HEROES TO
ACTUALLY DEFEAT ISRAEL'S ENEMIES,

THE SYRIANS. SEEK THE WORK FIRST
MACCABEES TO LEARN HIS REMARKABLE
STORIES.

IT ISN'T SURPRISING THAT A HERO
NAMED JUDAS WOULD WIND UP LEFT
OUT OF THE BIBLE. BUT IT WAS QUITE
A SHOCK THAT HEROD HAD HIS WIFE,
MIRIAM, BEHEADED. SOMETHING THE
JEWS WOULD NOT FORGET. AS MANY
KNOW, THE NAME MIRIAM TRANSLATES
TO MARY. A HEROIC NAME OR NAME OF
OTHER SIGNIFICANCE MEANS A LOT TO
PEOPLE, EVEN TODAY. MANY A TOWN

IN AMERICA IS CALLED LINCOLN, FOR EXAMPLE.

ANOTHER MIRIAM WAS BORN TO THE PRIESTLY TRIBE OF LEVI. WE WILL TALK MORE OF HER LATER. YOU CALL HER MARY. FIRST, LETS DISCUSS ANOTHER POINT OF SURVIVAL AND SUFFRAGE.

COVERT SPEECH

IT SHOULD NOT SURPRISE YOU THAT PAUL DREW A FISH IN THE SAND TO SAY HE WAS A NAZARENE, RATHER

THAN PROCLAIM ALOUD HE WAS ONE.
AMERICAN SLAVES SANG SPIRITUALS
INSPIRED BY THE EXODUS, OR THE
JEWISH SLAVE ESCAPE FROM EGYPT,
TO SIGNIFY THEIR DREAMS OF ESCAPE.
"STEAL AWAY'" WAS ONE OF THEM.
CROSS THE RIVER JORDAN ANOTHER.
SONGS OVERTLY RELIGIOUS, COVERTLY
SAYING WE PRAY TO ESCAPE THIS
SITUATION.

OLD TIMERS KNOW WHERE THE TERM
OFAY, FOR OPPRESSIVE WHITE BOSS
MAN, COMES FROM. IT COMES FROM

THE SPIRITUAL :GO DOWN MOSES,

WAY DOWN IN EGYPT LAND, TELL OLD

PHAROAH, LET MY PEOPLE GO. OLD

PHAROAH BECOMES OFAY. REMAINS

A SONG, BUT CARRIES A MESSAGE.

BECOMES A CODE WORD. FEW MODERN

BLACKS KNOW THE TERM OFAY, FEWER

STILL RECOGNIZE ITS ORIGIN.

IT THEREFORE SHOULDN'T SURPRISE

YOU THAT WE DON'T UNDERSTAND

THAT JESUS USED COVERT SPEECH

IN PUBLIC.WHEN HE MADE HIS

SPEECH FROM WHICH WE DERIVE THE

BEATTITUDES, THE THRONG CHEERED
WHEN HE PRONOUNCED THAT THE
MEEK WILL ENHEIRIT THE EARTH. WHY?
IF I HAVEN'T MENTIONED IT BEFORE,
THE MEEK IS ONE OF THE NICK NAMES
FOR THE MACCABEES, WHO RULED
FOR DECADES AFTER DEFEATING THE
SYRIANS.

IT WOULD COMFORT THE ENEMY TO
HEAR HIM PROCLAIM THAT WE SHOULD
REMAIN MEEK. BUT THAT ISN'T WHAT
HE WAS SAYING, OF COURSE.

IT SHOULD'T SURPRISE YOU THAT THE
JEWS ATE A PINCH OF BREAD RATHER
THAN BITE THE TWO FISH ON THE
COLLECTION PLATE PASSED AMONGST
THEM, DONATING WHEAT TO THE CAUSE
AS INSTRUCTED, SMALL BRONZE PENNY
COINS (OF HEROD'S TIME) CALLED
WHEATS. GRASPING AT THEIR FEET TO
EAT THE BITTER HERBS THERE IN THE
FIELD WHERE THEY STOOD. THE TWO
FISH REPRESENTED THE NATIONALITY
OF ISRAEL. THEY WOULD NOT BE
EATEN, PIECES, THE TWIN FISH. THE

CROWD WAS SATISFIED, MOREOVER,

FULFILLED.

THE HABIT OF SURVIVAL FOOD EATING

OF BITTER HERBS CAN BE FOUND IN

THE CEREMONY OF THE SATYR RITUAL.

JEWS ASK AT THE TABLE WHY MUST

TODAY WE HAVE BITTER HERBS FOR A

MEAL. THE ANSWER IS GIVEN BY THE

PARENT. IT REPRESENTS LOYALTY TOO.

JESUS SAID TO GIVE CAESARS COINS

TO CAESAR. THE HEROD WHEAT COINS

HAD THREE STRANDS OF WHEAT ON

THEM. HE ASKED FOR WHEAT TO MAKE

BREAD. BREAD STILL IS A NICKNAME

FOR MONEY.

WHEN OLD TIMERS CURSE THEY OFTEN

SAY: JESUS H., CHRIST!WHICH MAY

JUST GIVE YOU A CLUE TO JESUS'S

LAST NAME.

ONE OF THE LAST NAMES OF THE MEEK.

PAUL

PAUL WAS ORIGINALLY NAMED SAUL,

A PHILLISTINE TAX COLLECTOR. HE

BECAME A FOLLOWER OF CHRIST, AS
DID A NUMBER OF PHILLISTINES. THEY
WERE CALLED NAZARENES BY THE
ROMANS. AT LEAST THE ROMANS GOT
THAT RIGHT. PAUL ACTUALLY BECAME
THE FIRST POPE OR CHRISTIAN LEADER.
WHEN THE ROMANS CAPTURED HIM,
THEY BROUGHT HIM BY SHIP, BACK TO
ROME TO STAND TRIAL. THE SHIP SUNK,
BUT PAUL ARRIVED SAFELY. HE CUT OFF
ALL HIS HAIR. IN THE CAPITOL, IT WAS
ANNOUNCED "WE HAVE CAPTURED THE
LEADER OF THE NAZARENES!"

KOSHER AND COMMUNION

KOSHER IS THE SET OF DIETARY RULES OF THE JEWS IT IS NOT SIMPLE, BUT THE PRINCIPLES OF IT ARE.

LEADERS OF THE JEWS OBSERVED THAT PEOPLE PROSPER EATING CERTAIN FOODS, BUT THAT OTHER FOODS CAUSED ILLNESS OR DEATH THEMSELVES, OR IN COMBINATION WITH OTHER FOODS.

THE MOST DRAMATIC AND MEMORABLE RULE IS THAT PORK IS NOT KOSHER. LEADERS OBSERVED THAT PIGS ATE ANYTHING AND EVERYTHING. THAT THE FLESH DEVELOPED A GREEN RAINBOW PATINA. THAT TRICINOSIS WORMS DEVELOPED IN THE FLESH, AND IN ANY PERSON WHO ATE IT. THE EGYPTIANS ATE THE PORK, GOT SICK, SUFFERED LONG AND DIED IN AGONY. THE LONGER THEY LIVED, THE LARGER THE WORMS GOT. FILLING UP AND BLOATING THEIR BELLIES, GROWING LONG AND THICK LIKE SNAKES.

NOT EATING PORK THEN WAS VERY
VERY WISE PUBLIC INFORMATION. YOU
MAY ARGUE THAT THAT WAS BEFORE
PROPER REFRIGERATION, MEDICATION,
ETC, THAT THERE ARE NOW SAFER
STANDARDS FOR COOKING AND KEEPING
PORK, BUT FOR CENTURIES, THESE
STANDARDS DID NOT EXIST.

ICE IN THE DESERT?, NOT UNTIL THE
LAST 100 YEARS.

THE RULE OF SEPARATING DAIRY FROM MEAT IS ALSO INTERESTING. JEWS WHO LIVED NEAR THE SEA, GOT FRESH FISH. WHEN THEY WANTED MILK, THEY HAD TO TRAVEL HOURS AWAY TO THE FARMS WHERE CATTLE WERE KEPT.

EVEN CONSIDER RIDING A MULE OR DONKEY. A QUARTER HORSE CAN RUN FULL SPEED ONLY A QUARTER OF A MILE. A THOROUGHBRED, A FULL MILE. SO, IMAGINE A 20 MILE JOURNEY. TAKING 20 MINUTES BY CAR TODAY. ALL DAY, BACK THEN. BY FOOT, A BIG

UNDERTAKING. GETTING TO THE POINT,

WEDDING DAIRY WITH FISH MEANT ONE

OF THE ITEMS, MORE THAN LIKELY,

WOULD SPOIL. GIVEN THE TIME IT TOOK

TO REACH THE OTHER. MEAT TO DAIRY,

DAIRY TO MEAT.

IT WAS FORBIDDEN TO COOK MEAT IN

MILK. SOON FORBIDDEN TO HAVE THEM

ON THE SAME PLATE, POT OR SINK.

EATING CERTAIN SEAFOOD, AND MEAT

WITH CLOVEN HOOVES, SIMILARLY

BECAME FORBIDDEN.

KOSHER BUTCHERY STEMS FROM PRIMITIVE KNOWLEDGE THAT BLOOD REMAINING IN A MEAT ACCELERATES SPOILAGE. ONE REASON WHY FUNERAL MORTICIANS DRAIN BLOOD FROM CORPSES. ANIMALS ALLOWED TO BLEED OUT, OVERTIME, BEFORE THE HEART STOPPED PUMPING IT, LEFT A FLESH LESS LIKELY TO SPOIL FAST.

BY NOW YOU MAY ASK :WHY BRING UP KOSHER IN THIS WORK? THE ANSWER IS, JESUS WAS AND IS, A JEW, NO MORE

LIKELY TO EAT HAM AT A TABLE THAN
ANY OTHER JEW OF HIS TIME.

THE POINT IS, YOU HAVE A TRADITION
THAT YOU FORGET IS BIGOTED. THE
TRADITION COUCHED IN HATRED OF
JEWS, THE TRADITION OF EATING HAM
AT EASTER, AS A REBUKE AGAINST
THE JEWS WHO VOTED FOR HIS
CRUCIFIXION. THIS IS NOT AGAINST THE
PORK INDUSTRY.

JUST REMEMBER AS YOU BOW YOUR
HEAD AT THE EASTER FEAST, HE WOULD

NOT SIT DOWN WITH YOU AT A PORK
FEST.

THERE IS ANOTHER SET OF TRADITIONS
YOU MUST BE AWARE OF, IF YOU ARE
TO UNDERSTAND THE NAZARENE STORY.
ANOTHER RULE NO JEW WOULD BREAK.
BURIAL RULES.

UNDERSTANDING THE RULES EXPLAINS
MUCH OF THE OVERLOOKED TRUTHS IN
THE STORY. JEWS HAD TO BE PREPARED
FOR BURIAL WITHIN 24 HRS. OF THEIR
DEMISE. THIS CUSTOM PREVAILS TODAY.

IT ORIGINATED WITH THE SIMPLE FACT
THAT BODIES DECAY AND SMELL IF ONE
WAITS TOO LONG. EMBALMING WAS NOT
A JEWISH TRADITION. YOU MAY RECALL

THAT JESUS'S FAMILY URGED HIM NOT
TO ENTER THE SEPULCRE OF LAZARUS,
WARNING "BY NOW, HE SMELLS ".

SECONDLY, JEWS HAD A STRONG
PREFERENCE TO BE BURIED

ON THEIR FAMILY LAND. THEIR FARM,
PLOT OR BUNKER. MANY HAD PRIVATE

HILLS ON THEIR LAND, EXCLUSIVELY FOR FAMILY BURIALS.

IT WAS AN INSULT TO BE BURIED IN A STRANGE PLACE. IT WAS FOR THESE REASONS THAT JESUS WAS LET OFF THE

CROSS EARLY. AFTER ONLY 8 HOURS ON THE CROSS, WHILE OTHERS WOULD REMAIN THERE FOR DAYS, AS A SIGN TO OTHERS TO OBEY AND BEWARE, UNTIL THE CROWS AND DECAY ATE AWAY THE FLESH.

JEWS WERE TO BE BURIED (AND STILL

ARE) WITHIN 24 HOURS OF THEIR

DEMISE. MOREOVER, PASSOVER WAS

THE FOLLOWING DAY OF JESUS'S

DEATH. THIS LEADS TO MY ASSERTION

THAT NO STRANGER CLAIMED HIS BODY,

THAT WOULD HAVE BEEN RIDICULOUS

FOR FAMILY TO LET HIM BE CARTED OFF

TO A STRANGER'S PLOT.

WE ARE TOLD THAT JOSEPH OF

ARIMETHEA, AND NICODEMUS CAME TO

CLAIM HIM. I SEARCHED IN VAIN FOR

A LAND CALLED ARIMETHEA. THERE

IS NONE, AND NEVER WAS. I LEARNED THAT THE TERM ARIMETHEA MEANS "OF A HIGH PLACE" JESUS WAS CLAIMED BY HIS OWN FATHER, A MEMBER OF THE SANHEDRIN, HIGH COUNCIL.

NICODEMUS CARRIED A BUNDLE OF HERBS AND ALOES, WEIGHING A HUNDRED WEIGHT TO THE CROSS. APPARENTLY A STRONG MAN. TODAY'S DICTIONARIES LISTS HIM AS A JEWISH LEADER WHO ASKED JESUS A QUESTION. OR A "MEEK" FOLLOWER OF JESUS.

FACT IS, WE KNOW WHAT MEEK MEANS
NOW. AND HE WAS THE KING OF
JUDAH, THE SOUTHERN KINGDOM OF
THE JEWISH COUNTRY. HE WAS ALSO
ACCORDING TO A BOOK DISCARDED BY
THE CHRISTIANS, CALLED "THE BOOK
OF NICODEMUS", THE L AWYER FOR
JESUS BEFORE THE SANHEDRIN AND
BEFORE PILATE. STRANGERS?, NO!
REMEMBER, JEWS WERE TO BE BURIED
HONORABLY ON THEIR OWN FAMILY
LAND. JOSEPH TOOK HIS SON THERE.

ON THE OTHER HAND, TO BE BURIED

IN A POTTER'S FIELD WAS A DISGRACE.

YOU WERE DISOWNED BY THE GESTURE.

WE HAVE POTTER'S FIELDS IN BOTH

COUNTRY AREAS AND BIG CITIES,

WHERE THE HOMELESS AND UNCLAIMED

ARE BURIED. THE NAME COMES FROM

A BARREN LAND WHERE POT MAKERS

THEW OUT DAMAGED GOODS, BROKEN

POTS, UNWANTED MERCHANDISE, ON

USELESS LAND.

IMAGINE TRYING TO WALK IN AN

OLD POTTER'S FIELD. OKAY, TO THE

POINT, INTERESTING TO ME IS THAT JUDAS ABANDONED HIS PAYMENT FOR THE SUPPOSED BETRAYAL OF JESUS, WHERE? EVENTUALIY, INTO A POTTER'S FIELD.

GAINING WEALTH WAS NOT HIS PURPOSE. DOING AS EXPECTED OF HIM, WAS. A MAN WITH A HEROES NAME WHO WOULD SACRIFICE HIS EVERLASTING REPUTATION AND NAME, FOR A PURPOSE.

WHY WAS THERE SUCH A NEED FOR A
SAVIOR, REQUIRING SACRIFICE OF LIVES?

1. IMAGINE LIVING IN A COUNTRY
WHERE WEEK BY WEEK, THOSE LIKE
YOU ARE HUNG ON CROSSES (OR
TREES), LINING PUBLIC STREETS,
LEFT THERE TO ROT. WOULD THAT
BE TERROR? WOULD THAT BE REASON
ENOUGH TO PRAY FOR A SAVIOR?

2. IMAGINE YOUR UNCLE, A MINISTER
OR PRIEST BEING STABBED BY THE
POLICE IN FRONT OF HIS CHURCH

ALTAR. JESUS PROTESTED THIS. THE PERSON WHO RAISED HIS MOTHER, ZACHARIAS WAS SO KILLED. NOT ONLY ZACHARIAS, BUT A TOTAL OF 80 RABBIS WERE SO MURDERED BY HEROD'S MEN. 80 CHURCH LEADERS! ALL FOR REFUSING TO ALLOW THE IMAGE OF CAESAR TO BE HUNG ON THE TEMPLE WALLS. EVERY COMMUNITY WAS DEVASTATED BY THE MURDERS, BUT IT ISN'T MENTIONED IN THE BIBLE, EXCEPT BY JESUS HIMSELF.

3. NOT ONLY WERE THEIR LEADERS KILLED, BUT ISRAEL HAD FOREIGN KINGS, AND THEY REQUIRED A RELIGIOUS, JEWISH KING TO FEEL WHOLE.

4. LET ME BRING TO YOUR ATTENTION THAT WHILE WE SWOON OVER THE BIRTH OF JESUS, AT THE BEAUTIFUL SCENE OF THE NATIVITY WITH THREE WISE MEN AND MANGER ANIMALS LOOKING ON, HUNDREDS OF INFANTS WERE BEING MURDERED, SNATCHED FROM THEIR MOTHER'S ARMS. NECKS

TWISTED, HEARTS SLICED AS EASY

AS BUTTER,WITH SHORT KNIVES OF

HEROD.EACH AN INDIVIDUAL MURDER,

REQUIRING MUCH BLOOD WORK,

WALKING, BREAKING OF DOORS,

FIGHTING WITH PARENTS, MUCH

OUTRAGE, MUCH HATRED.

MUCH SORROW AND PRAYER FOR A

HERO TO COME.

ADD TO THIS, THE MURDER OF THEIR

PRINCESS OF THE HASMONEAN LINE,

BY HEROD, THE MURDER OF MIRIAM.

IMAGINE IF THIS WERE NOT ONLY YOUR
HOME TOWN, BUT, YOUR IMMEDIATE
FAMILY.

COMMUNION

JEWS HAD COMMUNION FIRST, STILL
USE IT TODAY. ORIGINALLY, SACRIFICED
MEAT WAS PLACED ON THE ALTAR
THE TEMPLE. AT THE FOUR CORNERS
OF THE ALTAR TOP WERE THE ALTAR
HORNS, TO HOLD UP THE GRATE WHICH
HELD THE MEAT ABOVE THE COALS
OR WOOD. AFTER THE CEREMONY,

A SELECTED CITIZEN WOULD SPEAK

OF FAITH OR COMMUNITY ISSUES.

WE DIDN'T EVEN INVENT BARBEQUE.

JESUS'S CEREMONY ONLY REPLACED

THE ANIMAL SACRIFICE. IT STILL

CERTIFIES OUR FAITH IN GOD VIA

CEREMONY OR RENEWAL.

JUBILATION

WE TEND TO SEE ORTHODOX JEWS AS

STAID AND QUIET.

THE TRUTH IS GOD TOLD THEM TO MAKE A JOYFUL NOISE UNTO HIM.

THEY DANCE AND SHOUT AND SING WITH JOYFUL HEARTS, AS HARD AS OUR CONCEPT OF HOLY ROLLERS, AND OTHERS WHO FEEL AND SHOW "THE SPIRIT".

FATHERHOOD

AS YOU WILL READ LATER, JESUS DIDN'T DIRECTLY SAY HE WAS THE ONLY SON OF GOD. HE SAID HE WAS THE

SON OF MAN. ADAM WAS FIRST MAN
AND IT IS HIS NAME, "MAN" PRIOR TO
HIS TRIAL, HE DIRECTED HIS DISCIPLES
TO SAY A PRAYER THAT BEGINS "OUR
FATHER WHICH ART IN HEAVEN" "NOT
JESUS'S FATHER". GOD CREATED, OR
FATHERED ADAM. MAN, FATHER OF ALL
MANKIND. WE ALL ARE DESCENDANTS.

THE PHILLISTINES

THE FIRST I HEARD OF THE
PHILLSTINES, I QUICKLY FORGOT THEM.
THIS WAS A MISTAKE. I KNEW THAT

SAMSON FOUGHT THEM WITH MUCH

SUCCESS, BUT THAT YET AND STILL

THEY RULED ISRAEL. SAMSON WAS A

REVOLUTIONARY. THE SAMARITANS,

ALSO DISLIKED BY THE JEWS IMPRESSED

ME MORE WITH ONE GOOD ACT THAN

ALL THE STORY OF THE PHILLISTINES.

BUT THEIR STORY IS SPECIAL TO THE

NAZARENE HISTORY

THE INTERRUPTION OF THE JEWISH

HISTORY, WAS WHEN BABYLON CARTED

AWAY THE JEWS AS SLAVES HOME WITH

THEM. IT IS AN INTERRUPTION NOTED IN THE ANCESTRY OF JESUS HIMSELF.

WHILE THE JEWS WERE AWAY, THE PHILLISTINES REMAINED, AND KEPT MUCH OF THE JEWISH TRADITIONS. THEY EVEN CALLED THEMSELVES JEWS.

WHEN THE JEWS RETURNED AND LOOKED FOR THEIR LAND AND BUSINESSES, THEY FOUND PHILLISTINES TAKING THOSE, THEIR NAME AND RELIGION. MUCH MORE HATRED INSUED.

THE PHILLISTINES WERE AN ADMIXTURE
OF PHOENICIANS AND THE ARMY OF
ALEXANDER THE GREAT. MOSTLY FROM
AN ISLAND CALLED CRETE. THESE
PEOPLE WERE HATED WORLD WIDE.
WHY?

WHEN ROME CONQUERED ANOTHER
PHOENICIAN/CRETE / TOWN IN
NORTHERN AFRICA, CALLED
CARTHAGE, THE ROMANS AT HOME
CHEERED:"CARTHAGA DELENDA
EST!"(CARTHAGE IS DESTROYED!)WHY?
NOT JUST OUT OF ENVY OF THE

GREATER MERCHANT SAILING ABILITIES
AND TRADE THEY ACCOMPLISHED
WORLD WIDE, NOT JUST BEACAUSE A
COUNRY WAS WON OVER, BUT BECAUSE
THESE PEOPLE HAD A CEREMONY
Where THEY KILLED THEIR YOUNG AS
SACRIFICE. BURIAL GROUNDS IN THE
HOLY LAND AND CARTHAGE RECENTLY
UNEARTHED THIS FACT. THESE
CRETIANS ALSO WERE THE REASON GOD
GAVE CANAAN OVER TO THE JEWS,
AND ADVISED ALL OF THE POPULATION
WAS TO BE KILLED AND NO GOODS OR
BOOTY, NO SLAVES TO BE TAKEN.

THE SPIES SENT BY JOSHUA TO LEARN

THE CITY OF CANAAN MUST HAVE

WITNESSED THIS HORROR. FUELING

THEIR ZEAL TO EXTINGUISH ALL LIFE

THERE. THESE PEOPLE, IF YOU KNOW

THE STORY OF CRETE, WERE ALSO BULL

DANCERS AND BULL WORSHIPPERS. THE

TAURUS - HORN -ENEMY SYMBOLISM.

BULL CEREMONIES THAT EVENTUALLY

LED TO BULL FIGHTING IN SEVERAL

LANDS.

YET AND STILL, THE JEWS COULD NOT
BE IMMUNE TO THE PHILLISTINES. IN
FACT, THE WRITTEN LANGUAGE OF
THE JEWS COMES DIRECTLY FROM
THE PHILLISTINES. THE ALPHABET
ALEPH TO TAU CAME FROM THEM. THE
COMMERCIAL ABILITIES CAME FROM
THEM.

THEY WERE THE WORLDS SUPREME
TRADERS, ASSIMILATING LANGUAGES
AND CULTURES AS THEY TRAVELLED.
THEY GAVE THE JEWS THEIR LOGOS.
THE BIBLE BEGINS, IN THE BEGINNING

WAS THE WORD, "LOGOS" AND THE
WORD WAS OF GOD.

THIS WAS MISINTERPRETED, JUST AS
JESUS THE NAZARENE IS NOW CALLED
JESUS OF NAZARETH.

JESUS'S FATHER HAD TO DEAL
WITH TRAVELLING MEN, PROBABLY
PHILLISTINES IF HE PLIED HIS TRADE TO
SEVERAL NATIONS. JESUS PROBABLY
TRAVELLED WITH HIM. WE KNOW HE
LIVED FIRST IN AFRICA.

JESUS HAD TO TRAVEL NORTH WITH HIS DAD IF HE WAS TO PROVE HE HAD WALKED ON WATER (ICE). AN UNHEARD OF THING IN AFRICA OR MIDDLE EAST. JOSEPH OF ARIMETHEA IS REPORTED BY SOME TO HAVE TRAVELLED TO AND SETTLED IN ENGLAND. A LAND NO STRANGER TO ICE AND SNOW.

ISAIAH

THE PROPHECY OF THE MESSIAH

JESUS MADE TWO EARLY SPEECHES.
ONE AS A CHILD WHERE HE TOLD THE
PHARISSEES AND SADDUCEES AND
SCRIBES "WHY BE SURPRISED THAT
I AM ABOUT MY FATHER'S WORK"
THEY WERE DUMBFOUNDED BY HIS
KNOWLEDGE OF THE SCRIPTURES.
SECOND WAS HIS COMING OF AGE
SPEECH, WHERE HE READ FROM THE
BOOK OF ISAIAH AND SAID "YOU
NOW SEE HIS PROPHECY FULFILLED."
HIS FATHER'S WORK WAS OF THE
SANHEDRIN COUNCIL.

ISAIAH'S WRITINGS WERE HIS GUIDELINE

FOR FULFILLING THE PROPHECY. BUT

YOU MUST EXAMINE WHAT ISAIAH

EXACTLY SAID.

ISAIAH WROTE :"TO A MAIDEN WILL

BE BORN A REMARKABLE BIRTH. AND

HIS NAME WILL BE EMMANUEL, THE

MESHIHU (MESSIAH).

THIS PUZZLED ME. THE NEW BIBLE SAYS

TO A VIRGIN, NOT MAIDEN.

AND WHY NOT JESUS, OR THE OTHER VERSIONS OF JESUS:JESSE OR YESHUA, WHICH IS JOSHUA? THIS SEEMING FAILURE OF PROPHECY LED ME TO THREE SOLUTIONS.

MARY WAS A MAIDEN OF THE TEMPLE BETROVED TO JOSEPH. JEWISH MARRIAGE IS TWO PART. BETROTHAL IS HALF OF IT. FULL MARRIAGE IS THE SECOND HALF, BUT STILL THEY ARE bound TO EACH OTHER, IN THE BETROTHAL STAGE. MAIDEN WAS CHANGED TO ABSURDLY, VIRGIN. SHE

DID INDEED STOP BEING A MAIDEN
WHEN SHE WAS FULLY MARRIED.

ISAIAH CALLED FOR A REMARKABLE
BIRTH. REMAKABLE, NOT VIRGIN.

WHAT IS A REMARKABLE
BIRTH?CAESARIAN? TWINS? TWIN FISH
OF PIECES? ENOUGH SPECULATION,
NOT VIRGIN BIRTH HOWEVER.

AS FAR AS EMMANUEL GOES. JESUS
NEVERSAYS HE IS THE SOLE SON OF
GOD. HE SAYS INSTEAD "I AM THE SON

OF MAN". OUT OF MAN COMES TO
BE EMMANUEL. ADAM WAS THE FIRST
CREATED SON OF GOD.

HIS NAME ALTERNATELY, IS ...MAN.
ACCORDING TO THE JEWISH
DICTIONARY.

JESUS FOLLOWS THE ISAIAH SCRiPT OF
THE MESSIAH TO THE LETTER, EVEN
ENTERING JERUSALEM ON A DONKEY
AS ISAIAH FORETOLD. DURING THE
40 DAYS IN THE WILDERNESS, JESUS

CONSULTED WITH ISAIAH (RECOUNTED, STUDIED,EXAMINED THE SCRIPT).

SLAVES AND AFRICANS

MANY OF THE SLAVES THAT LEFT AFRICA WITH MOSES WERE NOT JEWISH, SOME WERE HITTITES, PRIOR MORTAL ENEMIES OF THE EGYPTIANS IN AFRICA. SOLOMAN SON OF DAVID, ANCESTOR OF JESUS, WAS AFRICAN, HIS MOTHER A HITTITE. THE POLISH MADONNA IS BLACK.CHECK YOUR

EGYPTIAN ANTHROPOLOGY BOOKS FOR

IMAGES OF HITTITES.

CARPENTER

OUR BIBLE LISTS JOSEPH AS A

CARPENTER. AN ANCESTER, JUDAS

MACCABEUS, WAS CALLED THE

HAMMERER. THIS IS MY OPINION

ONLY, BUT TO ME,CAR-PENTER

MEANS CHARIOT MAKER. THERE IS NO

HOME MADE IN ISRAEL (CHECK YOUR

PHOTO COLLECTION OF THE HOLY

LANDS)MADE OF WOOD. NO NEED OF

TRAVELING CARPENTERS IN THE MID

EAST.

BUT EGYPT MADE THE BEST CHARIOTS.

JOSEPH LIVED THERE. WHEN PAUL

CAME TO THE ISLAND OF CYPRUS,

THE PEOPLE WORSHIPPED THOR, THE

GOD THAT SWUNG A HAMMER. THE

CRUCIFIXES AROUND DISCIPLES'S NECKS

APPEARED LIKE THE THOR HAMMERS

CYPRIOTS WORE AROUND THEIR

NECKS, HELPING GAIN AN INROAD FOR

CHRISTIANITY. DO NOT IGNORE THOR.

HE NAMED OUR THURSDAY, HIS WIFE

WEDNES IS THE PRIOR DAY.

THE MOON DAY AND SUN DAY ARE IN

THERE TOO.

ZACHARIAS

IF YOU EXAMINE EVERY WORD JESUS

SAID IN THE NEW TEASTAMENT, YOU

WILL FIND THAT ZACHARIAS IS ONE OF

THE FEW PERSONS JESUS CRIES FOUL

ABOUT, HIS MURDER BY THE ROMANS.

HE WAS MORE THAN A RABBI KILLED

BY THE ROMANS. HE RAISED JESUS'S

MOTHER IN HIS TEMPLE. HE HAD HER

EDUCATED, AND TRAINED TO WEAVE

THE TEMPLE VEILS OR CURTAINS.

BOTH HE AND MARY'S FATHER WERE

CHALLENGED BY THE INABILITY

TO HAVE CHILDREN. JOACHIM HAD

BEEN EMBARRASSED AT TEMPLE BY A

PRIEST WHO SAID IT WAS A SHAMEFUL

FAILURE NOT TO HAVE CHILDREN. THAT

GOD HAD INSISTED WE JEWS HAVE

CHILDREN.

ALTHOUGH HE WAS WELL TO DO AND
HAD BROUGHT MUCH TO sacrifice, TO
THE TEMPLE, HE LEFT FEELING SHAMED
AND A NEIGHBORHOOD FAILURE. GOD
ORDERED JEWS TO BE FRUITFUL AND
MULTIPLY.

ANNA, JOACHIM'S WIFE, WENT TO
HER SERVANT FOR CONSOLATION. THE
SLAVE OFFEREED HER HER HAT OR
VEIL. SOMEHOW
SHE BECAME PREGNANT, AND A CHILD
WAS BORN TO THE HOUSEHOLD.

IN THAT DAY YOUR SERVANT WAS BOTH
YOUR PROPERTY, BUT MORESO, PART
OF YOUR FAMILY. A CHILD BORN TO
YOUR SLAVE WAS YOUR CHILD.

SLAVES NURSED ALL THE MASTERS
CHILDREN AS THEY WOULD THEIR OWN.

ZACHARIAS ALSO HAD NO CHILD WITH
MARY'S COUSIN, ELIZABETH. SOMEHOW
HE FOUND A SOLUTION TOO. HE
COULDN'T SPEAK UNTIL THE CHILD WAS
BORN, AND THEY ASKED HIM WHAT WAS

THE CHILD TO BE CALLED. HE NAMED HIM JOHN, WHO WE LEARN GREW UP TO BE CALLED THE BAPTIST.

JOACHIM AND ANNA PROMISED THEIR CHILD TO SERVICE AT THE TEMPLE IF SHE WERE BORN, SO MARY, PROBABLY WELL FED AND CUTE, AT AGE THREE, WAS LED UP THE TEMPLE STAIRS, WEARING HER TINY SANDALS NO DOUBT FILLED WITH HONOUR TO BE SO CHOSEN.

WHEN MARY WAS GROWN (13 WAS MARRIAGE AGE THEN BECAUSE MANY PEOPLE DIED BY AGE 40), A CEREMONY WAS HELD WHERE THE PRIEST WOULD ASK THE ELIGIBLE MEN OF THE PARISH TO LINE UP AND THE SHOULDER THAT A DOVE LANDED UPON, WOULD BE THE CHOSEN GROOM. INSTEAD OF A DOVE, THE STAFF JOSEPH HELD REPORTEDLY BLOOMED WITH A FLOWER AT THE TOP. HE WAS CHOSEN.

MARY VISITED HER COUSIN, ELIZABETH
AND DISCUSSED THE FACT THAT THEY
WERE BOTH WITH CHILD TO COME.

LATER, WHEN THEIR CHILDREN MET,
ONE BAPTIZED THE OTHER, BUT SAID
IT SHOULD BE YOU BAPTIZING ME, HE
HAD BEFORE BEEN ASKED "JOHN, ARE
YOU THE MESSIAH? HE SAID "I AM SENT
BEFORE THE MESSIAH,HE WILL BAPTIZE
NOT WITH WATER, BUT WITH FIRE."

JESUS LATER SAID "I AM THE ALPHA
AND OMEGA" ATLEAST THAT IS WHAT

THE GREEKS SAID HE SAID. THE LAST LETTER OF THE JEWISH ALPHABET IS TAU, THE FIRST IS ALEPH. BUT THE MESSAGE IS HE REPRESENTS THE FIRST MAN AND THE LAST. THE BEGINNING AND THE END. ADAM AND, JESUS'S RETURN. OR EVEN MORE ACCURATE, THE FIRST CONTRACT MADE WITH GOD AND THE LAST ONE.

JOSHUA

JESUS WAS NAMED AFTER JOSHUA. REMEMBER THE JEWISH ALPHABET

SPELL JEHOVAH AS YHWH,

PRONOUNCES IT YAHWEH. IT IS EASY

FOR NAMES TO BE RE-WRITTEN

DIFFERENTLY. JOSHUA WAS THE

SECOND TO USE FIRE, FIRST WAS

MOSES. MOSES HAD SHEPHERDED A

FLOCK IN THE LAND OF MIDIAN, PRIOR

TO HIS RETURN TO EGYPT TO LEAD

THE EXODUS. WHEN THE ESCAPING

JEWS TRESSPASSED ON THE MIDIANITES

LAND, THE MIDIANITES KILLED AND

SCATTERED MANY OF THEM USING FIRE

AS A WEAPON.

MOSES DECIDED TO RETURN THE
FAVOR, AND WHILE THE MIDIANITES
SLEPT, HAD FIRE THROWN INTO THEIR
CAVES. MOST WERE KILLED BY SMOKE
AND FIRE, THE REST FLEEING THE FIRE,
BY THE JEWS.

JOSHUA ADOPTED THIS METHOD AS
HIS OWN. GOD ORDERED JOSHUA TO
CIRCLE THE TOWN OF JERICHO 7 TIMES,
HAVE HIS TROOPS YELL, BEAT DRUMS
AND BLOW TRUMPETS. HE ORDERED
THE JEWS TO CARRY OIL IN VESSELS,
WITH TORCHES. THELAST CIRCUIT

OF THE CAMP, THE STORY SAYS THE
WALLS CAME TUMBLING DOWN. MUCH
MORE LIKELY, THE WOODEN GATES
WERE BURNT DOWN SUCCESSFULLY
BY THE JEWS. THE INHABITANTS
HAVING NO DEFENSE AGAINST FIRE-
TORCHES THROWN OVER THE GATES.
NO DEFENSE AGAINST THE SMOKE.
TERRIFIED BY THE LATE NIGHT YELLING
BEATING OF DRUMS AND TRUMPETS,
SEEMINGLY EVERYWHERE AROUND THE
TOWN, WERE DEVASTATED.

NOTE, THE EIGHTH TIME JOSHUA

CAME BY FIRE. JESUS IS TO BAPTIZE IN

THE END BY FIRE. JESUS'S NUMBER IS

EIGHT.

THIS TERROR TACTIC WAS RECENTLY

USED BY THE FEDERAL POLICE

SURROUNDING AN AMERICAN CAMP OF

DIFFERING RELIGION.

LOUD ROCK MUSIC AND LOUDSPEAKERS

YELLED THRU THE NIGHT. AND IT ALL

ENDED WITH THE PLACE DESTROYED BY

FIRE.

A FAMOUS JEWISH HOLIDAY

CELEBRATES MIRACULOUS RESERVE

OF OIL BEING GRANTED BY GOD FOR

THEIR LAMPS. I SUBMIT OIL WAS A

TOOL OF OTHER USE BY THEIR TROOPS

DEFENDING THEIR LAND. A SECRET

WEAPON.

EXCAVATIONS OF JERICHO IN THE PAST

TEN YEARS DISCOVERED THAT THE

WALLS DUG UP WERE BURNT. THAT ALL

DWELLINGS WERE DESTROYED SAVE

ONE WITH A FLAT ROOF, NEAR THE

APPARENT FRONT GATES. PERHAPS THE ONE HOME SPARED BY THE TROOPS AS PROMISED TO THE HARLOT WHO HID JOSHUA'S SPIES FROM THE POLICE. SHE TOLD THEM IF DISCOVERED BY THE POLICE, OUT AT NIGHT, THEY WOULD BE KILLED. THEY KEPT THEIR PROMISE TO SPARE HER AND HER HOME.

SO NOW YOU KNOW THE MEANING OF THE FIRE NEXT TIME.

ADAM

THE FIRST MAN WAS ADAM. IN HEBREW IT IS WRITTEN LIKE "DON". IT TRANSLATES TO MAN.

WHEN ADAM AND EVE COMMITTED THE FIRST SIN, WHICH I SUGGEST WAS EMULATING OTHER ANIMALS AND KILLING OTHER BEINGS FOR FOOD, GOD TOLD THEM IF THEY WANTED TO HAVE FREE WILL, THEY WOULD HAVE TO LIVE BY THEIR WITS AND NO LONGER DEPEND ON THE FRUITS HIS

GARDEN PROVIDED, FREELY. THEY

WERE BANISHED FROM THE GARDENS.

THEY SOUGHT A CAVE FOR SHELTER.

NIGHTTIME CAME FOR THE FIRST TIME.

ADAM AND EVE WERE TERRIFIED,

FEELING GOD NO LONGER WAS THERE.

GOD TOLD THEM 'HAVE FAITH IN ME

THAT I AM ALWAYS HERE AND THAT THE

LIGHT WILL RETURN." THEY PROMISED,

THEY SLEPT, AND IN THE MORNING

THE SUN RETURNED. AS GIFT FOR THE

FAITH IN HIM, GOD GAVE ADAM THREE

GIFTS : GOLD, FRANKINCENSE, AND

MYRR. (READ ISAIAH FOR THIS RATHER

REMARKABLLE ACCOUNT.)THIS WAS
THE FIRST COVENANT WITH MAN, OR
CONTRACT OF FAITH IN GOD.

GOD MADE THE EARTH IN SEVEN DAYS.
JOSHUA CIRCLED THE WALLS OF
JERICHO SEVEN TIMES. THE EIGHTH DAY
IS THAT OF JESUS.

SPECULATE WITH ME WHAT THE
GIFTS WERE SYMBOLIC OF.GOLD.
WEALTH, POWER, THE KING TREASURE
OR CROWN. INCENSE.BURNED BY
RABBIS, PRIESTS, EVEN THE POPE,

FROM AN URN SWUNG IN CEREMONIES FROM A CHAIN OR ROPE. RELIGIOUS LEADERSHIP. MYRR, A GUM RESIN MIXED TO GIVE AS COMFORTING DRINK TO NEW MOTHERS, A HEALING POTION.SO WE HAVE KING, TEACHER AND COMFORTER GIFTS.

THE VEILS

IT MADE ME WONDER HOW OFTEN VEILS POPPED UP IN THE JESUS STORY.

MARY'S MOTHER'S SERVANT OFFERED

HER HER HAT (VEIL).

MARY IS INSTRUCTED HOW TO WEAVE

THE TEMPLE VEILS.

IN HEROD'S COURT, SALOME DOES

THE DANCE OF THE SEVEN VEILS.

REVEALING MORE OF HERSELF AS SHE

DISCARDS ONE AT A TIME.

THERE IS A DISCARDED BIBLE TALE OF

SALOME (A HASMONEAN THRU HER

MOTHER'S FAMILY HERODEOUS) IS

PRESENT WITH HER SERVANT AT THE

NATIVITY. THAT AT THE SERVANTS

PROMPTING SALOME TOUCHES JESUS

WITH HER CRIPPLED HAND, AND THE

HAND IS INSTANTLY HEALED. HEROD

HAD PROMISED UP TO HALF OF HIS

KINGDOM TO SALOME IF SHE DANCED

FOR HIM AND HIS COURT. SHE ASKED

INSTEAD FOR THE HEAD OF JOHN

THE BAPTIST, WHO HAD INSULTED HER

MOTHER BY REMARKING ON HEROD

MARRYING HIS BROTHER'S WIFE. COULD

SHE HAVE ACTUALLY BEEN AN AGENT

OF THE JEWS?

COULD SHE BE REALLY GRATEFUL TO

JESUS FOR HER HAND?COULD JOHN

THE BAPTIST ALREADY HAVE DIED.

THE AGE OF 33 WAS REALLY OLD BACK

THEN.

FINALLY, WHEN JESUS REPORTEDLY

DIED THERE WAS AND EARTHQUAKE

THAT TORE THE TEMPLE VEILS OR

CURTAINS. THERE ALSO WAS AN ECLIPSE

OF THE SUN. COULD WISE MEN FORSEE

ECLIPSES BACK THEN?

WOMEN WORE VEILS IN PUBLIC IN THE
MIDDLE EAST FOR MODESTY.

WHEN WESTERNERS MARRY, THE VEIL
IS LIFTED OF THE BRIDE. WHAT OTHER
VEILED MEANINGS ARE THERE IN THE
BIBLE? I'VE GIVEN YOU SEVERAL.

MARY MAGDALENE

BRIEFLY, MARY MAGDALENE IS KNOWN
ONLY BY A FEW FACTS :. 1. SHE WAS
NOT AN ADULTRESS, NOT THE ONE
SAVED BY JESUS FROM BEING STONED

BY A CROWD "JESUS SAYING HE WHO IS WITHOUT SIN, CAST THE FIRST STONE". 2. SHE FOLLOWED HIM, AND IS THE ONE WHOM HE CASTE DEVILS OUT FROM, BUT IS NEVER NAMED AS AN APOSTLE, YET SHE WAS INDEED ONE. SHE PREACHED IN ANOTHER LAND FOLLOWING HIS DEATH, AND SOME SAY BORE HIS SON, THE FISHER KING (PISCES KING). 3. SHE WAS PRESENT AT THE CRUCIFIXION, WHEN HIS DISCIPLES HAD ABANDONED HIM, AND THEY HID 4. SHE DISCOVERED HIM MISSING FROM HIS SEPULCRE, THE NEXT DAY.

BE AWARE THAT SHE IS THE ONLY

DISCIPLE WHOM JESUS KISSED. SHE

WASHED AND OILED HIS FEET. MANY

OF US ARE UNAWARE THAT THIS IS A

SEXUAL FUNCTION. SHOWING ONES

FEET TO A MAN FROM A MAN IS A

HOMOSEXUAL THREAT TO SEMITES.

TO THOSE WHO SEND COMMERCIALS

OVERSEAS TO ARABIC LANDS BEWARE

THE FLASHING OF FEET, BARE OR NOT,

IT'S RUDE TO SAY THE LEAST. I RECALL

A SCANDAL IN THE MIDEAST WHEN A US

REPRESENTATIVE WAS PHOTOGRAPHED

WITH HIS LEGS CROSSED SHOWING A HOLE IN HIS SHOE. AMERICANS FELT THE ARABS WERE OFFENDED BY THE WORN OUT SOLE, BUT IS WAS THE GESTURE OF SHOWING ONE,S FOOT TO ANOTHER MAN THAT WAS OFFENSIVE. THE MUSLIM GESTURE OF CLEANING ONE'S FEET AND CLEANSING THE NASAL PASSAGES ORIGINATED FROM THE NEED TO ENTER THE TEMPLES WITHOUT SAND IN THE NOSE AND ON THE FEET, FROM THE DESERT.

OTHER FOLLOWERS OF JESUS RESENTED THE CLOSENESS OF MARY MAGDELLEN, BUT READ THE LAST PAGE OF THE NEW TESTAMENT. IT SAYS "IT IS RIGHT THAT THE LAMB OF GOD SHOULD BE PERMITTED TO MARRY. " ALL JEWISH RABBIS ARE ENCOURAGED TO MARRY. IT IS NOT SOMETHING OF SHAME, BUT AN EXPECTATION. NORMAL MAN WANTS A PARTNER. IT IS NATURAL.

Printed in the United States
26858LVS00001B/178-195